ADVENTURES IN THE GREAT OUTDOORS

KAYAKING AND CANOEING

ROBYN HARDYMAN

WINDMILL BOOKS
New York

Published in 2014 by Windmill Books, An Imprint of Rosen Publishing
29 East 21st Street, New York, NY 10010

Produced for Windmill by Calcium Creative Ltd
Editor for Calcium Creative Ltd: Sarah Eason
US Editor: Sara Howell
Designer: Emma DeBanks

Pic credits: Cover: Shutterstock: Les Palenik. Inside: Shutterstock: Chrislofotos 22,
Vereshchagin Dmitry 9t, Le Do 11t, Martina Ebel 1, 28, Elena Elisseeva 6, 17, 19,
Falk 27t, 27m, 27b, James Stuart Griffith 29, Jorg Hackemann 7, Ammit Jack 9b,
Jakobradlgruber 4, Niv Koren 10, Les Palenik 25, Olga Lyubkina 5, 13, 21, Travis
Manley 11b, Monkey Business Images 12, Riekephotos 14, Conny Sjostrom 16, Plazas
i Subiros 8, Kalmatsuy Tatyana 18, Richard Thornton 15, Topseller 23, Oleg Zabielin
20, 24t, 24b, 26.

Publisher Cataloging Data

Hardyman, Robyn.
Kayaking and canoeing / by Robyn Hardyman.
p. cm. — (Adventures in the great outdoors)
Includes index.
ISBN 978-1-61533-750-7 (library binding) — ISBN 978-1-61533-817-7 (pbk.) —
ISBN 978-1-61533-818-4 (6-pack)
1. Canoes and canoeing — Juvenile literature. 2. Kayaking — Juvenile literature. I.
Hardyman, Robyn. II. Title.
GV784.3 H37 2014
797.122—dc23

Manufactured in the United States of America

CPSIA Compliance Information: Batch #BS13WM: For Further Information contact Windmill Books, New York, New York at 1-866-478-0556

Contents

Get on the Water!

Are you ready for an adventure on water? Wherever you live, you're not far from the water, whether it's a river, a lake, a lagoon, or even the ocean. Kayaking and canoeing are amazing fun and great ways to connect with nature.

Kayaks and canoes are both narrow, shallow boats that you propel with a **paddle**. The main difference between them is how they are paddled.

A kayak paddle is long and has a **blade** (the flat part that you pull through the water) at both ends. A canoe paddle is shorter, with a blade at just one end. There's more room for gear in a canoe and they tend to be more stable. Kayaks are easier to paddle solo and can generally go faster.

A kayak or canoe can take you places you'd never normally see.

Both kayaks and canoes can be paddled by one person or two.

The best way to start canoeing or kayaking is to learn the basic skills from an instructor before you head downstream. You'll find help at your local kayaking and canoeing club. The club may offer kayak and canoe rentals, classes, and even kayaking and canoeing vacations. Whether you want to quietly explore a lake or river or pit your skills against others in a competition, there's something for everyone in this exciting water sport.

Plan Your Trip

To make the most of your kayaking or canoeing trip, you need to do a little advance planning. If you've thought about where you're going, the weather conditions and, most important, the water conditions, you'll have a great trip.

Canoeing or kayaking in the river is different throughout the year. In summer, rivers usually have less water in them and flow more slowly. The Sun can burn, however, and there's a risk of dehydration if you don't drink plenty of water. In spring, it's great to see nature reawakening and in the fall the colors are awesome. At these times of year, you'll need good protection from the cold.

Whenever you go on your trip, it's important to find out about the water conditions. You don't want to set off down a gentle river only to find yourself on a ride through the rapids downstream! Your local kayaking store is a good place to get advice about the best locations.

Take a canoe out on a lake at different times of year to watch the landscape change with the seasons.

Kayaking at sea brings more challenges from the waves and the currents.

STAY SAFE!

Water can be dangerous. Before you start kayaking or canoeing, you must know how to swim.

A lake is a great place for beginners because it's much less likely to hold surprises than rivers or the ocean. If you have more experience, you can hit the waves and take your kayak out on the sea. Sea kayaking is more risky than kayaking on a lake. The sea is full of water **currents** that can carry you in directions you don't want to go, so this type of kayaking is definitely not for beginners.

Get the Gear

You can rent a kayak, canoe, and paddles until you're sure you want to buy your own. Whether you rent or buy your equipment, having the right clothing and other gear from the start of your trip will make it much safer and more fun.

First, you need to organize your clothes. You need to wear the right clothing to be comfortable as you kayak or canoe. Even on a hot day, the water can be pretty cold. If it gets through your clothes, you'll feel cold and uncomfortable. Keep warm with a wetsuit or an all-over waterproof suit with sealed cuffs. Add warm clothes underneath the waterproof suit for chilly days. Gloves are a good idea, too, as wet hands can get very cold. Last of all, you'll need waterproof shoes.

wetsuit

life vest

spray skirt

Always wear waterproof clothing.

The buoyancy aid is the single most important piece of equipment you need.

STAY SAFE!

Your helmet should cover the sides of your head and the back of your neck and fit well. Keep it buckled!

In a kayak, another great piece of gear is the spray skirt. This goes around your waist and attaches to the rim of the **cockpit**, to keep the water out of the boat. You'll want a dry bag, too, to carry items such as a first aid kit, water, phone, whistle, and dry clothes. The bag should attach securely to the boat.

Safety is a major concern on the water. You must wear a **buoyancy aid** such as a life vest, to help you float if you fall in. Always protect your head with a helmet. Riverbanks and beds can be rocky, and if you **capsize** you could hit your head. A helmet is a must if you're headed for fast-flowing water.

9

Kayaks and Canoes

When you're starting out, you'll probably use a basic kayak or canoe. However, there are many different shapes and designs of boat. Some are designed for speed, and some for stability. As you become more confident, choose the best one for the type of canoeing or kayaking you want to do.

One of the key design features in the boat is the shape of the bottom, or **keel**. A flat bottom makes the boat easy to turn quickly, but it is also less stable because it tips over easily and it's harder to balance in. Flat-bottom kayaks are therefore generally used for **white water** or fast-flowing conditions. A V-shaped keel makes the kayak more stable but harder to turn, so it is better for beginners.

STAY SAFE!

When you're new to the sport, use a two-person canoe or kayak with an adult.

The open design of the canoe makes it ideal for using on calmer water.

The pointed ends of the kayak make it easier to move in rough water.

The width and length of the boat are important, too. Long, narrow kayaks are more **streamlined** than shorter ones. This means they will keep moving through the water for longer after each stroke. These kayaks are also designed for touring, which makes them ideal if you're going a long distance. Canoes are wider than kayaks, and less suited to long distances. They're also open on top, so they are better for calm conditions when water is less likely to get in.

Paddles can be made of wood, metal, or plastic. Choose a paddle that is light and strong, so that it's not too tiring to use. Canoe paddles are more often made of wood than kayak paddles, because they are smaller and less heavy.

Kayak paddles have a blade at each end. They are light but strong.

Get Set

You've got the gear, you've chosen your boat, and you're ready to head for the water. Now you need to master some important skills to get safely afloat.

Kayaks and canoes are heavy, but if you learn how to carry them properly you won't hurt yourself. For a canoe, you will definitely need two people to carry it. Take one end of the boat each. Kayaks often have grab loops at each end to make it easy for two people to carry them. If you're carrying a kayak alone, put your arm inside it and slowly lift it up onto your shoulder. Be sure that your back takes most of the weight.

Your back should take the weight of your boat, not your shoulder.

Sitting Properly

To keep your muscles from becoming sore, learn how to sit correctly in your kayak before you put it in the water!

1 Carefully get into the boat, sit down, and be sure you are comfortable.

2 Adjust the back support so that you're not leaning back at all. Your chest should be slightly forward.

3 Place the balls of your feet on the foot pegs, with your toes pointing outward.

4 Adjust the pegs so that your knees are pointing upward and outward. Your legs should be in contact with the thigh braces on the kayak.

5 Rock the kayak from side to side, and lean backward and forward, to make sure you are comfortable. You should feel at one with the boat.

Explore This!

You will need:
- kayak
- grassy area

If you get your sitting position right you'll have a comfortable ride.

Launching

Even the most experienced kayakers and canoeists sometimes find it hard to get into and launch their boats. With practice and balance, though, you can make sure you don't get too wet!

You can launch a canoe or kayak from a beach, a jetty, or a riverbank. The technique is different for each location. It's best to practice in shallow water first, to perfect your balancing skills. Once you're confident, you can try launching from more extreme locations. Some kayakers can launch from a steep riverbank or jetty. First, they get in the boat, then they lean backward as the kayak dips right down into the water. Canoes cannot be launched this way because they'd fill with water!

Launching from a beach into shallow water is best for beginners.

Launch Off!

Follow these steps to launch a kayak from a shallow riverbank or jetty.

1 Put the kayak in the shallow water and stand alongside it.

2 Rest the paddle on the deck behind the cockpit, with one end still resting on the bank.

3 Grip the paddle at the edge of the cockpit with one hand. This will help to steady you as you climb into the boat.

4 Carefully climb in. Sit on the back of the cockpit first, then slide your bottom in.

5 Fasten the spray skirt if you are using one.

6 Bring the paddle around in front of you and then use it to push away from the bank.

You will need:
- kayak
- paddle
- spray skirt (optional)

Start paddling as you move away from the bank.

15

Use Your Paddles

It may sound odd, but there's a right way and a wrong way to hold the paddle when you're kayaking or canoeing. If you hold your paddle incorrectly, you'll put a strain on your body.

Most people hold a kayak paddle backward the first time they pick it up. However, this is incorrect and will result in less power in your stroke. Your paddle blade has a smooth side and a ridged side. Keep the smooth side facing you. This is the side to pull through the water.

The middle of the paddle is the **shaft**. If you're right handed, grip it in your right hand. This is your control grip, so it needs to be firm but not too tight. The other hand grips less tightly and slips around as you paddle on each side. Be sure that your hands are centered on the paddle and a little wider apart than your shoulders.

Take strokes on alternate sides of the boat to go straight forward.

To use a canoe paddle, first put your top hand on the top end of the paddle, so that when it's vertical your knuckles face the sky. Only your lower hand should grip the shaft of the paddle. Your two hands should be just over shoulder width apart. To go forward, take turns dipping in the single blade on either side of the boat, twisting from side to side as you do so.

Two people in a canoe take turns to paddle on each side of the canoe.

STAY SAFE!

Keep hold of your paddle at all times. You can't move your canoe or kayak without it!

Perfect Strokes

Whether you're kayaking or canoeing, there are three stages in each paddling stroke. First is the "catch," which is when the blade enters the water. Second is the "pull through the water," and third is the "recovery." This is when you lift the blade out of the water and prepare for the next stroke.

When you twist to take a stroke, be sure to turn your whole upper body, not just your shoulders. This gives more power to your strokes and spares you the pain of sore muscles.

Put the blade cleanly into the water ahead of your body, with its thin edge facing upward. Rotate your body and roll your wrist on the shaft to pull the blade through the water. In calm water, pull the blade back as far as the rear tip of the kayak if you can. Lift the blade out of the water and continue turning so that you're ready for a stroke on the other side.

When kayaking, the most important thing to remember is to keep your hands in line with your shoulders.

In a canoe, switch arms so that each arm takes a turn as the top arm to avoid putting stress on just one arm.

It's most efficient to paddle on the left side of the canoe when your right hand is on top of the paddle.

When canoeing, start by bringing your top hand up above your head, so that the shaft is almost vertical. Reach forward and put the blade in the water, keeping it upright. Pull with your bottom hand, and push with your top hand. This will move the blade in a straight line.

19

Turning and steering

Once you've mastered moving forward, you can start to learn how to change direction and turn around. To turn your canoe or kayak you use the forward and backward strokes and a stroke called the "sweep stroke."

The sweep stroke turns the boat away from the side on which you use it. Twist away from that side, then plant the blade in the water up by the **bow**. Use your core muscles to twist and turn the boat around the blade. Remove the blade from the water when it gets to the **stern**. To make a sharp turn, take a backward stroke. This is the forward stroke in reverse.

To turn around, paddle on only one side of the boat.

Draw Stroke

You'll need to use the "**draw stroke**" to move your boat sideways in the water, such as toward a bank. You use the same stroke for both kayaking and canoeing.

You will need:
- kayak or canoe
- paddle

1 Twist at the waist to face the direction in which you wish to move. If you want to move right, twist right. If you want to move left, twist left.

2 Reach out toward the water with the paddle blade. Your left hand should be at around eye level.

3 Put the paddle in the water as far from the boat as you can. It should be facing the side of the boat.

4 Pull the blade in toward the boat, but not touching the side.

5 Rotate the blade out of the water, toward the stern.

6 Repeat the stroke until you reach your destination.

STAY SAFE!

Don't push on the paddle when using a draw stroke, or you may capsize.

A draw stroke is used to move the boat sideways.

21

A Quick Exit

Being out on the water can be dangerous. You need to know how to get out of your kayak quickly if it overturns and you find yourself in the water.

First, you'll need to know how to keep yourself upright if your kayak starts to wobble. A "**brace stroke**" will set you straight when you're slightly overbalanced on one side. Sit upright holding the paddle. While keeping your hands low, lift your elbows almost to your shoulders. Keep your head over the boat. Lift the paddle on the side nearest the water, then bring the paddle down hard, flat onto the water surface. Flick yourself upright from the hips.

If you're starting to overbalance, a brace stroke can set you upright again.

It's essential to master your **wet-exit** from a kayak before you go on the river. Ask for help from an instructor or buddy.

If you overturn your kayak, don't panic! Bring your body "close to the deck." In other words, tuck yourself forward. This protects you from underwater obstacles and makes it easier to get your legs out of the kayak. Pull the toggle on the spray skirt to detach it. Push the kayak up, forward, and away from your legs. Be sure to grab your paddle when you come back to the surface. Swim to your kayak and grab it. Stay with it if you can, but the most important thing is to get to shore safely.

STAY SAFE!

If you're separated from your kayak or canoe, avoid underwater obstacles such as rocks or roots by floating on your back with your hands crossed over your chest.

23

white water

White-water kayaking or canoeing is the wildest experience you can have on the water. If you're brave enough to try it, it can be incredible!

White water is water that is full of air. It froths, churns, and swirls downriver very quickly. It's made white by rushing over rocks and other obstacles below the surface. These are a hazard for the paddler. White-water rivers are graded from 1 to 6, according to how hard and dangerous they are to paddle down. Even an expert paddler would find a grade 6 river a serious challenge.

Experienced paddlers can read the river for the safest course to take.

White-water canoeists in a **slalom** competition follow a twisting course between pairs of poles, or "gates."

White-water rivers can be narrow and deep, or broad and full of torrents. Before setting out, research the conditions you're likely to find. Ask experienced paddlers and look in books and on the Internet. It's essential to master the strokes to control your boat through the conditions you find. Experts also learn to "read" the surface of the river for what lies beneath. For example, V-shaped ripples pointing upstream are a sign of rocks below, so always avoid those. A **chute** is an area of smooth water in a white-water section and is usually the safest route through.

25

Ready to Roll

When you're white-water kayaking or canoeing, you're much more likely to capsize. There are several things you can do if this happens, but you'll need to practice them before you head to any white water.

You've hit a problem and you're about to turn over. With experience you'll learn how to "hip-snap" your boat back upright before you capsize. This uses your hips and core body muscles. If you've gone under, you must make a split-second decision whether to exit your kayak underwater or stay in it. Ideally, you'd turn the boat back upright without getting out.

If you exit, you can lose the kayak and paddle and will have to swim through dangerous water. You might be able to do a **"buddy roll,"** in which another kayak comes to your capsized boat. You hold onto the boat and pull yourself back upright.

If you overbalance too far, you'll go under!

Eskimo Roll

The **"Eskimo roll"** is a technique that a kayaker can use to flip his or her kayak without getting out of it.

1 Capsize the boat so you're upside down in the water.

2 Bring your head and body forward so you are as close to the boat as possible.

3 Position your paddle alongside the kayak, and reach your hands out of the water as high as you can.

4 Turn the paddle across the kayak bottom and reach your top arm as far over the kayak as possible.

5 Reach out with the lower arm to get the outer blade up to the surface.

6 Keep your head down on the shoulder of your lower arm.

7 Hip-snap back upright, pushing down on the paddle blade at the same time.

8 Stabilize yourself and don't lift your head up too quickly.

You will need:
- kayak • paddle
- calm, safe water or pool to practice in

STAY SAFE!
You must only attempt an Eskimo roll under adult supervision.

Every white-water kayaker will flip over at some time. The Eskimo roll is an essential skill to master.

27

Go Green

We all have a responsibility to keep our wild places safe and unspoiled for the future. That way, everyone can continue to enjoy them. Whatever your outdoor adventure, remember to respect the natural environment and try to make as little impact on it as you can.

Our rivers, lakes, and oceans are beautiful, and kayakers and canoeists need to keep them that way. If you're going on a canoeing adventure upriver, or exploring a lake, never drop anything into the water. Litter can seriously harm fish, birds, and other creatures living in or by the water. They might eat it or get tangled in it. Litter pollutes the water, too.

If you stop to picnic or camp on the bank be sure to pack up your litter and take it home with you. Be aware that some creatures make their homes on the riverbank. Don't get too close or disturb parents and their young with your boat.

Enjoy the nature all around you without disturbing it.

Be sure to take home everything you bring on your trip, including litter.

If you're an experienced kayaker or canoeist, and you enjoy launching directly from a steep bank or rocks, think about the terrain you're on. Be careful not to damage the wildlife around your boat. White-water paddling is more likely to threaten you than the wildlife, but try to grab your gear if you capsize and wet-exit. That way you won't leave it to pollute the water.

Glossary

blade (BLAYD) The wide flat part at the end of a paddle.

bow (BOW) The front end of a kayak or canoe.

brace stroke (BRAYS STROHK) The paddling stroke that helps you to keep upright after tilting to one side.

buddy roll (BUH-dee ROHL) When someone in another canoe comes to help you flip back upright after capsizing.

buoyancy aid (BOY-en-see AYD) An inflated waterproof jacket that helps you to float in water.

capsize (KAP-syz) To turn over so that you're in the water.

chute (SHOOT) A path of smooth, fast-flowing water.

cockpit (KOK-pit) The open part of a kayak that you sit in.

currents (KUR-ents) Movements in a body of water that can be fast-moving and unpredictable.

draw stroke (DRAW STROHK) The paddling stroke that moves a kayak or canoe sideways.

Eskimo roll (ES-kuh-moh ROHL) The technique for getting back upright in a kayak after capsizing, without getting out.

keel (KEEL) The underside of a boat.

paddle (PA-dul) The equipment used to propel a kayak or canoe, with a long handle, or shaft, and a blade at either one end or both ends.

shaft (SHAFT) The part of the paddle that you hold on to.

slalom (SLAH-lum) An event in which kayak or canoe racers navigate a series of gates along a whitewater course.

stern (STERN) The back end of a kayak or canoe.

streamlined (STREEM-lynd) Shaped to move efficiently through the water.

sweep stroke (SWEEP STROHK) A paddling stroke used for turning and steering.

wet-exit (WET-ek-sit) The technique for getting out of a kayak underwater after capsizing.

white water (WYT WAH-ter) Fast-moving, turbulent water.

Further Reading

Mason, Paul. *Kayaking and Canoeing: The World's Best Paddling Locations and Techniques*. Mankato, MN: Capstone Press, 2011.

Thorpe, Yvonne. *Canoeing and Kayaking*. Know Your Sport. North Mankato, MN: Sea to Sea Publications, 2011.

Young, Jeff C. *Running the Rapids: White-Water Rafting, Canoeing, and Kayaking*. Adrenaline Adventure. Minneapolis, MN: Checkerboard Books, 2011.

Websites

For web resources related to the subject of this book, go to: www.windmillbooks.com/weblinks and select this book's title.

Index